Copyright 2018

All rights reserved. No part of these pages, either text or image may be used for any purpose. Therefore, reproduction, modification, storage in a retrieval system or retransmission, in any form or by any means, electronic, mechanical or otherwise, is strictly prohibited without prior written permission.

This is a work of fiction. Names, characters, businesses, places, events, locales, and incidents are either the products of the author's imagination or used in a fictitious manner. Any resemblance to actual persons, living or dead, or actual events is purely coincidental.

Jonathan branch is the American author of some of American favorite short self-published children's books. He began writing poetry and teaching Pre algebra at the age of 18. He is a celebrated and established author and awarded writer by many. His book shows display his works at Barnes and noble, local book stores and toy stores in Princeton, New Jersey and in Hopewell, Virginia. Jonathan branch is a former firefighter and rescue squad member. He is also up for the African American world record for the title of most children's books. He speaks 3 languages and teaches GED courses online for displaced individuals who look up to him for guidance. He has spoken on the radio and has given many speeches all over the states. He has received numerous awards including the prudential youth leadership award, awards from Washington dc and was the former vice president of toast masters. Currently he is working on medical patents for children with physical therapy and bone cancer equipment for pediatric patients.

Welcome to Childbranch Books

We have written the best action and adventure books for children for years. So sit back and get ready to travel far away to rescue a princess or fight a dragon ....

Enjoy the magic ....

To all the parents that love to read our books at night to your lovely children......

Thank You

We will continue our great work in pursiut of great accomplishments. Our illustrators are from Italy, London and the Philippines. We have 235 bools to write so keep reading ......

Flowers and leaves were all over the streets and the neighborhood.

The news reporter came on TV. "Good evening fellow news fans. A category five hurricane is coming on the way.

Please stay indoors and lock up all valuables. This is going to be a big one." The TV shut off and then the power went out.

The flowerpots in the window began shaking.
They fell to the ground. The storm of the
century was coming.

Rufus the dog ran upstairs and hid under the bed. He was scared of all the frightening noises that were coming from outside.

The trees were scratching their branches on the window. Rufus shivered with fear.

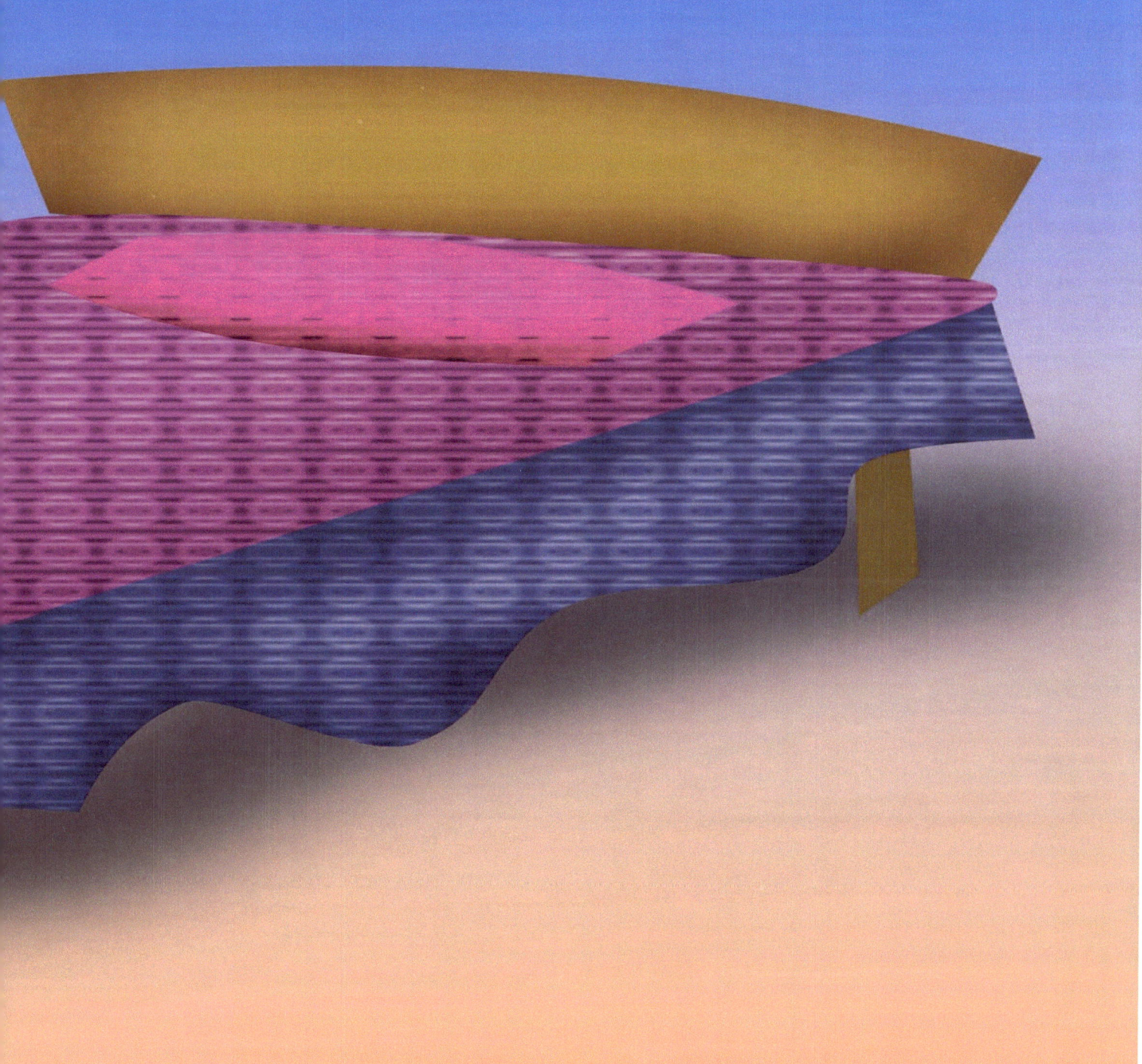

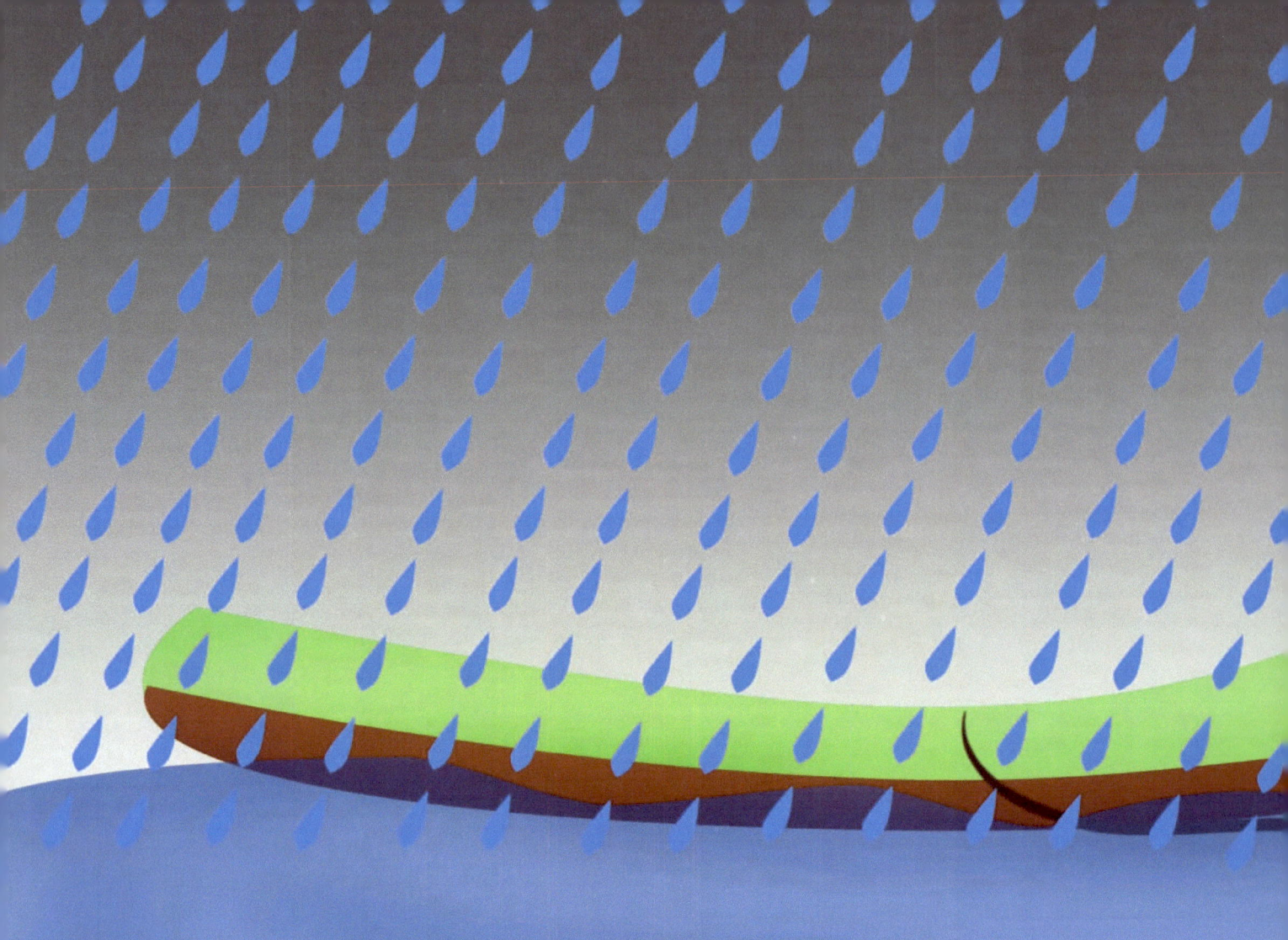

The sky turned gray. The canoe next door started to float! It was still attached to the pole in the ground. The flowers on the porch were soaked with water. It was coming and it would be bad.

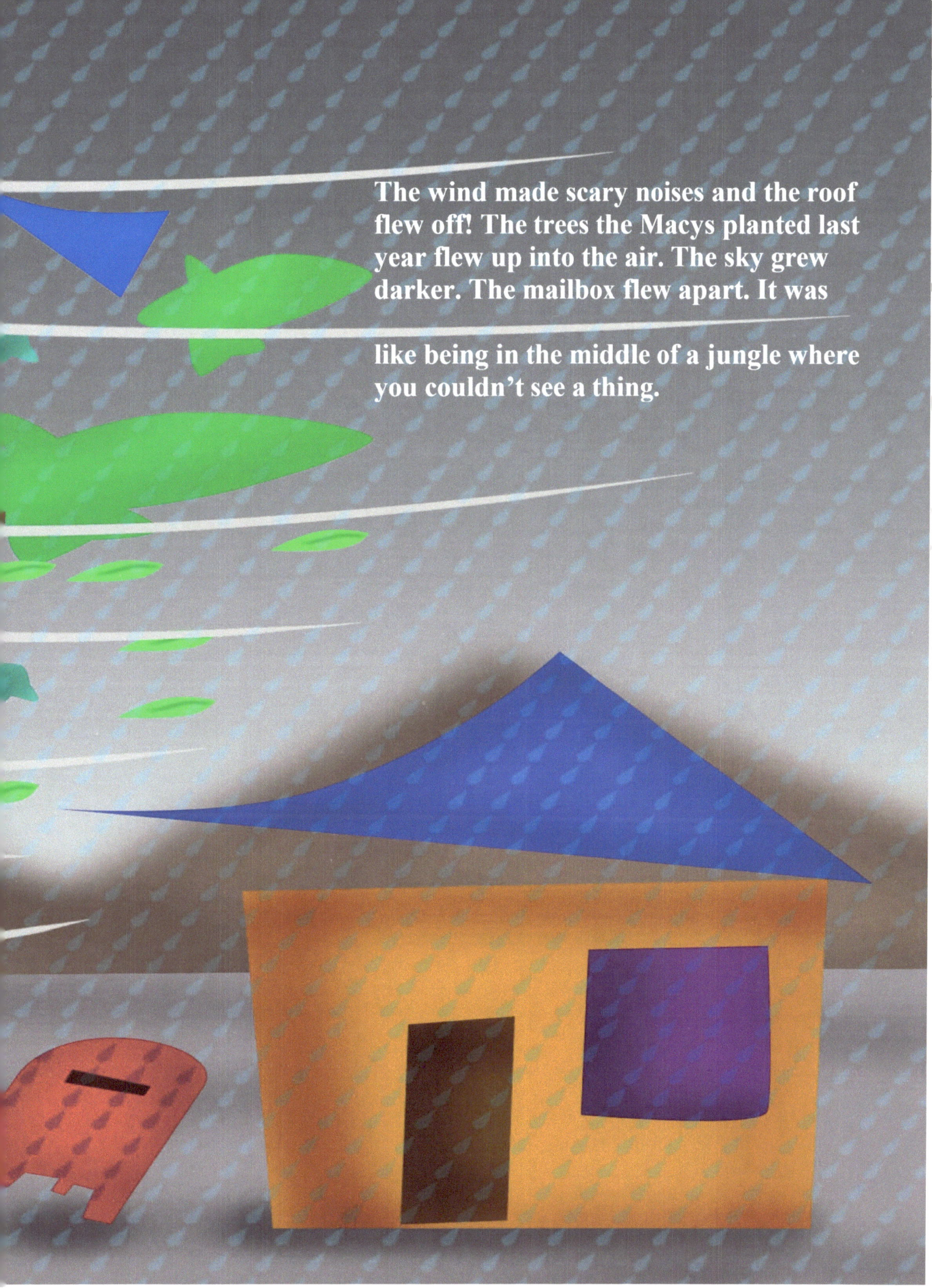

The wind made scary noises and the roof flew off! The trees the Macys planted last year flew up into the air. The sky grew darker. The mailbox flew apart. It was

like being in the middle of a jungle where you couldn't see a thing.

"Timmy get away from the window!" Timmy and his parents ran upstairs away from the glass. Then the windows broke. They smashed into a million pieces. The new Plexiglas window shattered all over the new dining room floor. The books were ruined. Water and hail flowed into the house.

The street grew more crowded with items. The rain made the soil loose and everything that was buried was coming apart. The stop sign and the yield sign were floating down the street at a tremendous speed. Everything from the auto body shop was gone.

"Somebody help me! Please!" Someone yelled. Timmy ran downstairs and looked across the street. There was a little girl hanging on a tree outside!

She was clinging on a branch for dear life.
Timmy ran out and swam to the tree
before she would be lost.

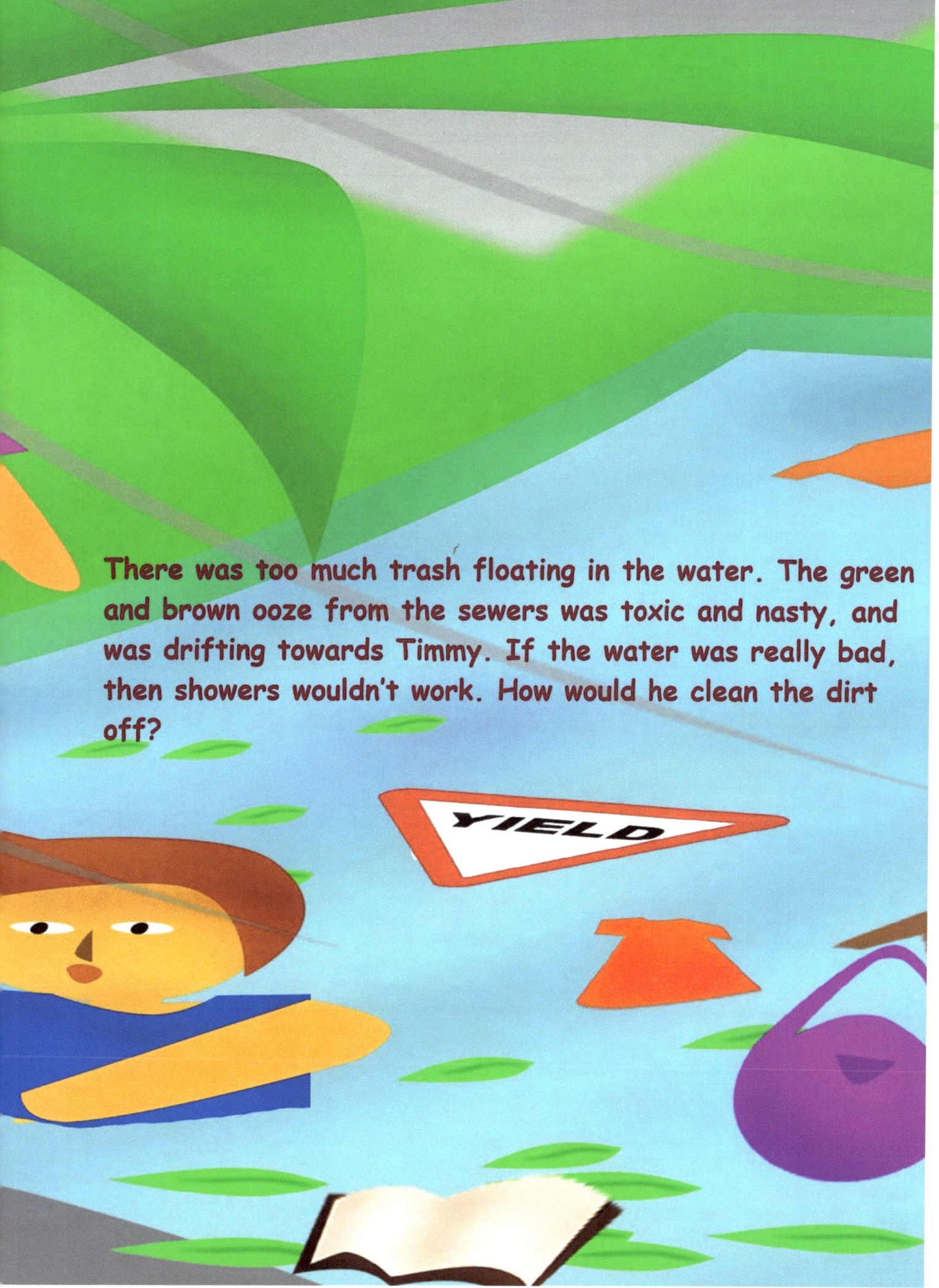

There was too much trash floating in the water. The green and brown ooze from the sewers was toxic and nasty, and was drifting towards Timmy. If the water was really bad, then showers wouldn't work. How would he clean the dirt off?

YIELD

Timmy brought her back to his house. They swam away from all the garbage and chaos. The skies started to clear up. "Thank you for rescuing me," she said.

"Sure," said Timmy. "What's your name?" "Myra," she replied. "I'm Timmy and this is my house. It's crazy out there." "Yeah it is."

They walked to the stadium down the street, which was the shelter for the whole town. Many people from the village were there too. Timmy took Myra to the cot in the corner and helped her into the bed. She was cold and wet.

Timmy got a first aid kit from the corner. He put a
band aid on her arm where she had gotten cut.
The cut was deep and she could be infected or worse...

Myra's dad came to her bedside and spoke to him. "Hello there, you must be Timmy." "Yes," Timmy replied. "I am. I saw her, and she needed my help so I brought her here." "Thank you Timmy," her dad said. "So listen, I know I'm nine, but could I take her to the movies?" "I just met you Timmy, not so fast," Myra's dad answered. "It was worth a try," he said, "but I do deserve it though," he added with a smile.

We would like to take the time to thank our amazing illustrators and editors

Edward Kos
Raymond Ariola
Amy foster
Clizia Brozzesi
Jhoiye Mendoza
Michele Paoluccci

Raymond Ariola passed away during the philippines storm. We will miss him greatly!

More Spectacular Books on the Way !!

 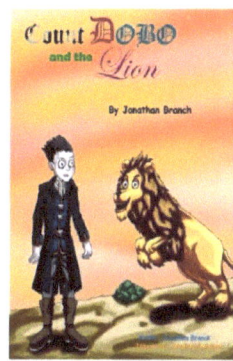  

   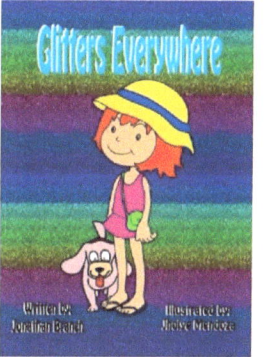

www.ingramcontent.com/pod-product-compliance
Lightning Source LLC
Chambersburg PA
CBHW041534280526
45792CB00004B/1497